WINE 101

WINE 101

A Brief Introduction to Wine

E. Terrence Woolf

ISBN: 978-1-956736-07-6 (Paperback Edition)
ISBN: 978-1-956736-08-3 (Hardcover Edition)
ISBN: 978-1-956736-06-9 (E-book Edition)

Book Ordering Information

Phone Number: 315 288-7939 ext. 1000 or 347-901-4920
Email: info@globalsummithouse.com
Global Summit House
www.globalsummithouse.com

Printed in the United States of America

INTRODUCTION

There are hundreds of books on wine available today, most of them written by people with far more expertise than this writer. The only excuse I have for writing this little guide, is that I have found that most of the good wine books contain so much information and detail about obscure wine that they completely overwhelm people who want to spend more time drinking wine than studying it. I have also encountered too many waiters who think Zinfandel is only a "blush" wine (a term I reserve for rosé which lacks any real flavor other than sugar), and I hope that perhaps some of those waiters may be willing to read a short description of some of the most commonly available wines in the United States, even if they have no interest in knowing the best vintages of Bordeaux.

For those wishing to quickly find a wine to go with dinner, I have inserted a table of suggested food-wine pairings at the end of this guide. Hundreds of grape varieties are used to make wine (not to mention wine made from strawberries, plums and other fruit) and there are many thousands of wine makers, each with his own distinctive style, so it would probably be impossible to taste all of them in a lifetime, much less write about them. As most American wine drinkers are somewhat familiar with wines named after the primary grape used in making the wine, this guide attempts to describe only the most common varietal wines sold in the United States.

Until the 1970's, the great majority of really good wine was made in France, and as a consequence, wines made in new wine growing regions in the United States, Australia, and South America were usually made from French grapes and given the French name of the primary variety of grape used to make the wine. Thus this guide to wine is organized by grape variety rather than by area of production. Since an understanding of wine made in places other than France requires some background knowledge of French wine, this guide covers the most common French grape varieties used in the United States along with a brief description of the French regions where the grapes originated. Admittedly, the selection is somewhat arbitrary and many excellent varieties have been omitted in the interest of keeping this guide reasonably brief.

In France, "terroir," the particular area where the grapes are grown, along with its soil type, vineyard slope, and climate, has been extremely important, and the grape varieties which will do well in a particular location have been discovered over several hundred years of making wine. In order to prevent fraud and insure the high quality of their wines, the French have established a complex system of regulation called the Appellation d'Origine Contrôlée, relating to the naming and labeling of wine and even governing the type of grape which must be used in a particular area if the wine maker desires to use the name of the area on his bottles. The United States in the 1970's established a similar system through federal regulation, and state laws may be even more strict.

Unlike in France, where the name of the grape varieties are often not revealed on the label (a notable exception being the wines of the Alsace region), in the United States, most fine wines are made primarily of a single grape variety and that variety is generally used on the label, usually under the name of the winery. The only thing important for a consumer to know is that if a wine claims to be from a particular area, at least 75% of the grapes used to make the wine were in fact grown in that area, and that, in order to use the name of a particular variety on the label, at least 75% of the wine must be of that variety.

WINE TASTING AND SERVING WINE WITH FOOD

The flavor of most food is enhanced greatly when served with a complimentary wine, and some food-wine parings are suggested at the end of this book. These suggestions are not rules of course, and you should always feel free to experiment without fear of appearing foolish or unsophisticated.

Ultimately, one can learn about wine only by tasting it. One method of tasting several types of wine is to have a regular wine tasting with friends with, for instance, each couple bringing a bottle of Pinot Noir with a cost of $15 - $30, and blind tasting each wine with food. Although some people argue that wine can be evaluated accurately only if food is limited to a few crackers to cleanse the palate between wines, I have found that some wines which are great with crackers are simply so tannic and heavy that they overwhelm almost any food that might be served with them.

However, cheese and crackers are usually good accompaniment for red or white wine at a wine tasting, as long as the cheese is not one of the very pungent varieties. Rich cheeses such as Brie go very well with crisp white wines such as Sauvignon Blanc and Pinot Gris.

However, selecting a food to be served with your wine at a wine tasting should not of course be limited to cheese and crackers - i.e. sparkling wines such as Champagne go particularly well with fresh oysters; and Cabernet Sauvignon and other red wines are very good when accompanied with dark chocolate.

It also must be remembered that wine contains alcohol. Nothing ruins a wine tasting group faster than having one of its members arrested for drunk driving or worse, injuring themselves or someone else in an event caused by alcohol. It is therefore advisable to pour only a few ounces and to serve food over a 2-3 hour period of time with the wine. Remember that you don't have to be "drunk" to be guilty of driving under the influence of alcohol – a DUI conviction requires only a .08 blood alcohol level (and in some cases even less) and some people with high tolerance don't exhibit obvious symptoms of being drunk until they reach levels of .15 or more. Blood alcohol levels depend on many factors including how fast the alcohol is consumed, whether it was consumed with food, the size of the person, and his rate of metabolism. Thus there is no rule for how much one can consume without reaching the .08 level. However, as a general guide, the average male might reach a .08 blood alcohol level by drinking four 6 ounce glasses of wine over a 2 hour period of time. A small woman might reach that level after only a couple of drinks. If there is any doubt, provide your guests with a spare couch or a cab ride if a designated driver is not at hand. If everyone wants to drink without worrying about driving, one option is to rent a limo to pick everyone up and take them home, or to use a service such as Uber.

Wine consumed in limited amounts with food will not cause a hangover in a normal person. However, if you have consumed too much wine, you may be able to prevent a hangover by taking three regular strength aspirin with two large glasses of water before going to bed.

Cost of course is a major consideration for most people, but very good wine can be obtained for less than $15 a bottle. Although some wines cost over $100 a bottle, most of them are not significantly better than wines costing less than half as much, although if you can afford it, there is certainly nothing wrong with drinking a $100 bottle of wine on a special occasion.

Most people can detect a noticeable difference in wine served in a proper wine glass and wine served in an ordinary glass. A good wine glass is smaller at the opening than in the portion below containing the wine. A stem prevents the drinker's hand from warming the wine (a result desired only when drinking Cognac or other brandies). In order to allow the wine to be aerated in the glass by swirling the glass in a circular motion, the glass should be filled only to about 1/3 of its capacity.

Corks are still used in most fine wine (although modern screw tops make corks unnecessary), and wine service traditions have been developed around the problems caused by using natural cork. After pulling the cork, the host should pour a small amount of the wine into his/her own glass before serving the guests in order that any small amounts of cork will be in the glass of the host. The host should smell the cork (particularly in the case of old red wine) in order to detect any evidence of oxidation, which can occur if the cork has dried out (a condition usually caused by failing to store wine on its side). A sour vinegar smell means the wine is probably not drinkable.

Next, the wine should be swirled around in the glass to release its aroma, and after smelling the wine, the host should take a small portion into his mouth, holding it there for a few moments in order to really taste the wine. Being assured that the wine is worthy of his/her guests, the host should proceed to serve the wine. The same procedure is used in restaurants serving fine wine, with the person ordering the wine playing the role of host.

Red wine which has not been filtered may have some sediment remaining in the bottom of the bottle. If serving an older red wine, it is a good idea to pour the wine into a decanter before serving in order to allow the wine to breathe, and to make sure that any sediment remains in the bottle. Although some people advise merely opening red wine a couple of hours before service to let it breathe, I doubt that exposing the top of the wine to an opening the size of a dime makes much difference to most people.

Red wine should usually be served at cool room temperature – about 55 - 65 degrees F. There are of course exceptions – some people enjoy Italian Chianti red wine served chilled with spaghetti.

Chardonnay, Viognier, and other full-bodied whites are best served at 45 - 50 degrees F. They should never be placed in an ice bucket as this will chill the wine too much and mask its flavor.

Sauvignon Blanc, Pinot Gris and other light bodied white wines, as well as semi-dry wines like Riesling and Chenin Blanc, can be chilled down to 35 - 40 degrees F in the refrigerator. However, almost all wines will lose flavor if served very cold. Thus even light bodied white wines are probably appreciated more if they are allowed to warm up slightly before serving.

Wine left over can be re-corked, or the top of the bottle sealed with one of the wine closing devices currently on the market. Red wine will sometimes last for more than a week after the bottle is opened, but white wine will usually lose its flavor if not consumed within a day or two.

PURCHASING AND STORING WINE

Does Vintage Matter?

Yes. Vintage, the year the grapes were harvested, matters a great deal when purchasing French and other European wines because in many years, cold conditions may delay the grapes from ripening or rain may affect the quality of the grapes. Although the United States and California in particular has a more consistent climate and therefore there is less emphasis on vintage, wine grapes grown in California will still vary considerably from one year to the next, and in any given area certain vintages are simply recognized as superior to others. The practice of many restaurants of not listing the vintage of their wines means that one should assume that the wines come from very recent vintages.

Unfortunately, only relatively expensive restaurants are likely to have older vintages available for purchase, and if they do, such wines are usually extremely expensive. If you want to insure having a good bottle of older vintage wine with a dinner in a restaurant, you should ask about the "corkage" fee charged by the restaurant for opening and serving wine from your cellar.

This guide does not recommend particular wines for the reason that a wine may be great one year and mediocre in the next vintage, and most wines are simply not available in all areas. The best advice is to find a good wine merchant who can guide you to the best values and make recommendations concerning top quality wine you may wish to add to your cellar.

It is helpful to consider ratings of wine by publications such as Wine Spectator, or respected tasters like Robert Parker, but make sure the rating applies to the wine you are thinking of buying. Some less than honest wine merchants will put a rating from another vintage on a vintage which was not rated as well. Also keep in mind that the ratings are usually just the opinion of one person who may have tasted dozens of different wines that day. The ratings are rarely verified by having other tasters evaluate the wine. Moreover, every taster has his own prejudices, and thus a wine which one taster may give a 95 might be given a 90 by someone else.

That being said, you will rarely get less than a very good bottle of wine if you select one rated 87 or higher by a reputable person or publication (the 100 point scale has become the most common rating tool). The best values are often found among those wines rated 87-89, since the wines rated 90 or higher typically command significantly higher prices. It must also be remembered that not every vintage of every wine can be rated and a good wine merchant can steer you to excellent wine which has not been rated.

Storing Wine

Everyone interested in wine can create at least a small wine cellar for storage of those wines one wishes to save for special occasions or to develop further flavors by aging in the bottle after the wine is released. Most high quality red wines, and some white, will be considerably better after a few years resting in a cellar, especially if the cellar is kept cool and dark.

Remember that light and heat are the enemies of wine, and wine should not be stored in an open wine rack in the bar or the kitchen, although such racks are okay for keeping wine which will be consumed within a few months. The ideal cellar is a basement or refrigerated wine cellar kept at 50 – 60 degrees F. If you do not have a basement or wine refrigerator, a box under a bed or in a closet where the temperature is consistent and will not exceed 70 degrees F, will do.

The length of time to age wine cannot be given with any certainty, but I think that high tannin red wine such as Cabernet Sauvignon, Syrah, Petite Sirah and Zinfandel, should be aged a minimum of five years after the vintage. Although some Chardonnay can be improved with a couple of years of bottle age in the cellar, I have found that most white wines lose their fruit flavor as they age and I recommend drinking them within a few months of purchase.

This advice applies as well to Champagne and other sparkling wines, with the exception of vintage Champagne, which may be excellent after a dozen years or more of bottle age.

Wine sealed with a cork should be stored on its side, never on its bottom, in order to keep the cork from drying out and allowing too much air to come in contact with the wine. Genuine cork (made from the bark of Cork Oak trees) is rarely used these days so that the ritual of smelling the cork after the waiter has withdrawn it from the bottle, in order to make sure the wine has not been ruined by a bad cork, is now rarely necessary. Screw tops have been developed which do as good a job as real cork, and they are preferable in my opinion to artificial corks which are often very hard to remove from the bottle.

Most drinkers of wine which has been aged in the bottle for many years have had the experience of opening an expensive wine only to find that it has been spoiled by an infected or dried cork, and one must accept the risk of wine going bad if one wants to have the benefit of drinking some top-quality red wine which has been aged for many years in the bottle. When planning a special dinner around a wine which has been aged for a substantial period of time (i.e. longer than ten years), it is good to have a backup wine to serve in the event the older wine has gone bad.

MAJOR WINE VARIETIES

As has been noted, the great majority of fine wine was once produced in France, and and therefore wine growers in other countries usually selected French grape varieties as the basis for their wines. Although there are many more wine varieties to choose from today than a decade earlier, some top Italian wine makers have recently switched from the Italian Sangiovese grape and started using French varieties such as Cabernet Sauvignon and Merlot, and Spanish producers are using those French Bordeaux grapes in lieu of Spanish varieties such as Tempranillo.

I have found it helpful in understanding the major wine varieties to refer to a map of France showing the location of the six wine producing areas which have been the most important in spreading their grape varieties to the United States and throughout the world:

Bordeaux (red area in southwest France), responsible for red wines such as Cabernet Sauvignon and Merlot, Malbec, and other red grape varieties, and white wines from Sauvignon Blanc;

Burgundy (blue area in central eastern France), for red wines from Pinot Noir, and whites from Chardonnay;

Alsace (gray area in the far east of France, next to Germany), for white wines such as Pinot Gris, Pinot Blanc, Gewürztraminer, and Riesling;

Champagne (orange area east of Paris) for Champagne;

Loire River Valley (green area west of Paris) for white wines from Sauvignon Blanc and Chenin Blanc; and

Rhone River Valley (purple area in southern France) for white wine from Viognier and blends and red wine from Syrah and blends.

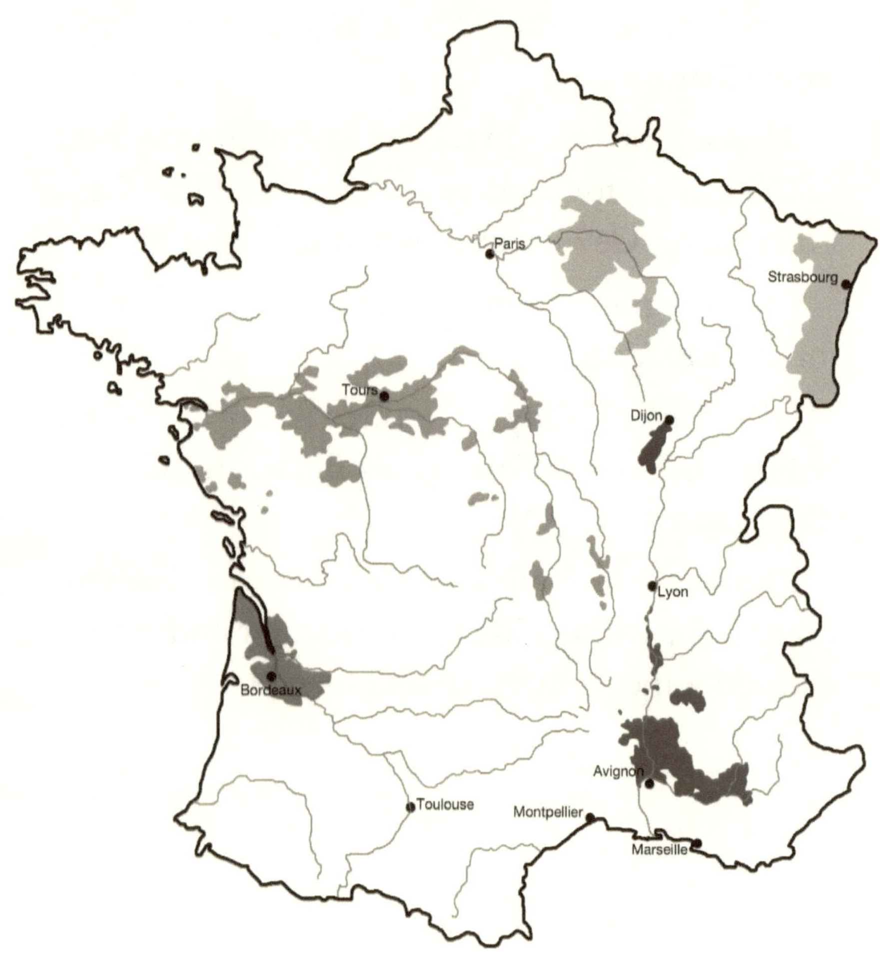

Paris
Strasbourg
Tours
Dijon
Lyon
Bordeaux
Avignon
Toulouse
Montpellier
Marseille

FRENCH WINE REGIONS			
Region	Color	Location	Major Grape Varieties Used
Bordeaux		Southwest France	**Red:** Cabernet Sauvignon, Merlot, Cabernet Franc, Malbec **White:** Sauvignon Blanc, Semillon
Burgundy		Eastern France	**Red:** Pinot Noir, Gamey **White:** Chardonnay
Champagne		Northeastern France	**Red:** Pinot Noir (for both white and rosé Champagne) **White:** Chardonnay
Loire		Northwestern France	**White:** Sauvignon Blanc, Chenin Blanc
Rhone		Southeastern France	**Red:** Syrah, Grenache **White:** Viognier, Roussanne, Marsanne
Alsace		Eastern France	**White:** Pinot Gris, Pinot Blanc Riesling, Gewürztraminer

During the last 30 years, the United States, Italy, Spain, Chile, Argentina, and even South Africa have joined France in making top quality wine. (Although particularly the Italians would argue that Italy has always made top quality wines and in Dumas' novel, The Three Musketeers, the musketeers were fond of Spanish red.)

In the United States, California is recognized as the state producing the greatest quantity of fine wine, particularly in the Napa Valley, Sonoma County, and the Central Coast. However, many states other than California produce excellent wine – Oregon is noted for Pinot Noir, Washington produces excellent Cabernet Sauvignon and it may surprise some people that producers in states as diverse as New Mexico, Texas, Indiana, and even New York make very good wine.

CALIFORNIA WINE REGIONS

The above map of California reflects the most important and well known wine producing regions in the state – Napa (brown), Sonoma (red) and the Central Coast (blue).

In these areas of California, located near the coast, cool evenings moderate daytime summer heat, making it much easier to produce fine wine than in areas like California's hot Central Valley, although some very good wines are made in wineries around Fresno, Madera and in the Sierra Foothills east of Sacramento.

In the United States, almost every varietal is produced in most wine growing areas. Thus although the Napa Valley is best known for its Cabernet Sauvignon and Chardonnay, it also produces excellent Pinot Noir and Sauvignon Blanc as well as less well known varieties such as Petite Sirah. Sonoma County, the source of some of the best Pinot Noir, also is known for producing very high quality Cabernet Sauvignon, Chardonnay and Syrah; while the wineries in the Central Coast area are best known for red Rhone style wines, they also produce superb Pinot Noir and Zinfandel. Oregon is known for excellent Pinot Noir and Washington for Cabernet

Sauvignon, but both of these states also produce many other varieties.

Since the 1970's wines produced in other countries have increased in quality to a point where they are now often equivalent to the best wines of France. In 1976, a British wine merchant who had been visiting California's Napa Valley, brought to Paris for a blind tasting six Chardonnay wines and six Cabernet Sauvignon wines. After arranging for top French wine experts to judge the wines, he added four French white Burgundies (made from Chardonnay grapes) and four of the best red wines of Bordeaux (made from Cabernet Sauvignon grapes). To everyone's surprise, the French judges awarded the most points in the white wine category to California's Chateaux Montelena, and the most points in the red wine category to California's Stag's Leap winery. Although it was only one tasting and the wines were selected arbitrarily by one person, the tasting established that California wineries could produce wines which were as good as any in the world.

Following are brief descriptions of some of the most commonly available wines, organized generally from sparkling wines to the lightest bodied white wines, and finally to the most full bodied reds and concluding with a brief description of sweet dessert wines.

24

Champagne and Other Sparkling Wine

Champagne is a "sparkling" (carbonated) wine produced when wine is allowed to undergo a secondary fermentation, creating bubbles. Real Champagne comes only from the Champagne area of France, which is located east of the city of Paris.

Producers of real Champagne naturally resented the use of the name to describe sparkling wines produced in other areas, and U.S. law now prohibits use of the name Champagne on labels of wines produced outside Champagne, France, except for some California producers who have been given "grandfather" status – if they had used the word "Champagne" on their labels before 2006, they may continue to use the term "California Champagne."

Almost all producers of good sparkling wine in California and other U.S. states simply label their "sparkling wine" by that term, although many people continue to describe any sparkling wine as "Champagne." Sparkling wine produced in other areas of France may be called "Cremant"; while sparkling wine produced in other countries may be given other names, e.g. in Italy, "Spumante," and in Spain "Cava."

Real Champagne is made from Chardonnay (a white grape variety), and/or Pinot Noir or Pinot Meunier (red skinned grapes which have white juice), and that tradition has been followed in California. Rosé sparkling wine is produced from Pinot Noir or Pinot Meunier grapes which have been allowed longer contact between the red skin and the white juice of the grapes.

With respect to sweetness, "Brut" is the style of most Champagne – it is very dry, although some sugar has been added. Slightly sweeter Champagne is labeled "Extra Dry" and "Demi-Sec" is very sweet, although the term "Demi-Sec" actually means "Semi-Dry."

Most sparkling wine is best consumed when young, although some sparkling wine, particularly vintage Champagne, can be excellent even after several years of aging in the bottle. Sparkling wines should be served in a tall, tulip shaped glass in order to emphasize the effect of the bubbles. It should never be served in wide mouthed cocktail glasses, even if the legend is true that the shape of such glasses is based on the breast of Marie Antoinette.

Pinot Gris / Pinot Grigio

Pinot Gris (pronounced "peno gree") is a dry, crisp white wine made in the Alsace region of France, as well as in Italy, America and other countries. It is usually inexpensive – very good Pinot Gris is often available for less than $10 a bottle.

The Pinot Gris grape variety probably originated in the Burgundy region of France, then made its way to the Alsace region of France by way of Eastern Europe. The grapes are blue -grey ("gris" means "grey" in French) and many believe that Pinot Gris produced in Alsace results in a richer and more flavorful wine than that produced elsewhere.

Pinot Gris in Alsace may be made in a dry style, or the grapes may be left on the vines longer in order to increase sugar to levels necessary to make very sweet dessert wine.

In Italy the grape is called Pinot Grigio - California vintners use both names. The wine is often made in a very light style, and it is sometimes blended with Chardonnay or other white grape varieties to make a more full-bodied wine. Pinot Gris is crisp and has good acid, which makes it a good choice to serve with shellfish or delicate fish such as sole, snapper and cod.

Pinot Blanc

The best examples of Pinot Blanc ("peno blonk"), a white wine which is somewhat richer and fuller bodied than Pinot Gris, also come from Alsace, France, but very good Pinot Blanc is also made in California and in other areas of the United States. It goes well with pork, chicken, and richer fish dishes such as salmon and shellfish.

Sauvignon Blanc

Sauvignon Blanc ("so veen yohn blonk") - "blanc" meaning "white," originated in the Bordeaux region of Southwestern France (red area on the map) and is the variety primarily used to make the white wines of Bordeaux, where it is often blended with Semillon. It is also a primary variety used in the Loire Valley which is located in the Northwest area of France (green area on the map). In addition to Sauvignon Blanc from Bordeaux and the Loire Valley, excellent Sauvignon Blanc is produced in the United States, Australia, and New Zealand. Some Sauvignon Blanc wines have a slightly grassy flavor, particularly those from Australia.

Sauvignon Blanc grapes are light green and like Pinot Gris, are usually used to make a dry, crisp white wine, although also like Pinot Gris, Sauvignon Blanc grapes can be left on the vine to produce very sweet dessert wine.

Although some French wines made from Sauvignon Blanc, such as those made from the Graves area of Bordeaux can be very expensive (some exceeding $100 a bottle), excellent Sauvignon blanc wines can be obtained from California, New Zealand, Australia, and France for $7 - $10 a bottle.

Like Pinot Gris, Sauvignon Blanc is a light crisp white wine, but it usually has more body and flavor than Pinot Gris, and thus goes with a wider variety of food including fish, cheese and light poultry dishes.

Gewürztraminer

Gewürztraminer is another white wine whose best examples come from the Alsace region of France. The grape lends a spice note to wines made from it. In Alsace, the wine is usually dry, but California Gewürztraminer is often made in a semi-sweet style, with a relatively high residual sugar level. Both styles go particularly well with ham and other pork dishes, and the sweeter style is very good with oriental food.

Riesling

Although the French make superb dry and sweet white rieslings in Alsace , the variety is best known for dry ("trocken"), semi-sweet and sweet German and Austrian wine. In the United States and other countries, Riesling is usually made in a semi-sweet style. Like Gewürztraminer, it goes well with ham and pork, and is a good choice to accompany Asian cuisine. Riesling is often made in a lower alcohol version which makes an excellent aperitif and summer everyday drinking wine.

Chenin Blanc

Chenin Blanc is grown in the Loire Valley and other areas of France, as well as in California.

Chenin Blanc produced in the area surrounding Vouvray is usually available in most wine shops. It is a crisp white wine with a sweet edge, which goes particularly well with Asian cuisine, as well as with chicken, pork and ham. Although it is often produced in a semi-sweet style, Chenin Blanc can also be made quite dry. The dry style goes well with all types of fish and light chicken dishes.

Viognier

Viognier ("vwah neeay") is a flavorful, dry white wine best known in France for the excellent wines produced at Chateau Grillet and Condrieu in the Rhone Valley of Southeast France (yellow area on map). In recent years, California and other areas have also produced excellent Viognier wine. Like full-bodied Chardonnay, it pairs well with chicken, pork, turkey and stronger fish dishes such as salmon and swordfish.

Chardonnay

Chardonnay originated in the Burgundy region of Eastern France. Although most Americans think of Burgundy as a red wine, the white Burgundy wine made from the green skinned Chardonnay grape is equally rare and expensive.

It is used to make what many consider the finest white wine in the world – the great white Burgundies produced in Chablis and Montrachet. The grape was successfully introduced to most of the wine producing areas of the world, and excellent Chardonnay wine is made in California, Washington, Oregon, and Australia.

There are two main styles of Chardonnay – a crisp and light bodied style which results from little or no aging in oak barrels and where the wine has not undergone a secondary malolactic fermentation; and a more full-bodied "buttery" style wine which is the result of the wine being subject to malolactic fermentation. Malolactic fermentation is the process of taking the harsher malic acid (the tart acid found in a green apple) in a wine and converting it to a softer lactic acid (the acid in milk and butter).

Most American Chardonnay is grown in warm climates and is subjected to malolactic fermentation, resulting in a rich, buttery and full-bodied style. Chardonnay grown in cool climates, such as Chablis which is in the far north of the Burgundy region of France, is usually made without malolactic fermentation or aging in oak barrels, resulting in a crisp and tart white wine. (Real Chablis tastes nothing like the cheap generic white wine which was once sold in the United States under the name "Chablis.")

The lighter, crisp version of Chardonnay, like other light and dry white wine, such as Pinot Gris and Sauvignon Blanc, goes well with delicate fish and shellfish, while the full bodied or buttery style is a better choice with salmon, chicken, veal and pork.

Chardonnay is one of the few white wines which can benefit from aging in the bottle. However this benefit is generally available only with top quality Chardonnay which tends to be quite expensive, at $50 a bottle and up. Even when an expensive Chardonnay is allowed to age in your cellar, there is no guarantee that it will not taste like vinegar if left too long in the bottle.

ROSÉ WINE

Most red grapes have white juice, and red wine results because the skin is allowed to remain with the crushed grapes. If the skin is removed shortly after the grapes are crushed, rosé wine results. Rosé (rose-ay) wine is usually a pink or very light red in color, and can be very flavorful. Some rosé wine has a bad reputation because it is made in a style which results in a wine which is overly sweet and lacking any fruit flavor. This "blush" wine, sometimes sold as "white Zinfandel", should not be confused with the very good rosé wine now being made from Zinfandel, Syrah and other red grape varieties.

Rosé wine can be made from almost any variety of red grape, so one can purchase rosé Cabernet Sauvignon, rosé Syrah, etc. Because the skins are left in contact with the white juice for a relatively brief period, rose wines usually do not taste anything like the full red variety, but they can nevertheless be excellent wines, particularly for drinking on a hot summer day when a red wine would be oppressive.

Very good rosé wine is made in the south of France and in Central California, as well as in Napa and Sonoma counties, and it goes particularly well with ham, turkey, chicken and salmon. It does not have the ability to age like red wine, but is usually inexpensive (unless it is rosé Champagne or other rosé sparkling wine, which usually costs as much as, and sometimes considerably more than, the golden hued variety of Champagne).

RED WINE

Pinot Noir

Pinot Noir ("peno nwaa") is perhaps the most versatile and flavorful red wine, with the exception perhaps of Cabernet Sauvignon. It is medium bodied without the heavy tannins found in Cabernet Sauvignon and most other red wines, and can therefore be enjoyed when quite young, although the best Pinot Noir can age for many years. (Tannins are compounds found in most plants including the skin of red wine grapes. It allows red wine to age well but creates a dry and astringent feeling in the mouth when the wine is young. The thin skin of Pinot Noir grapes results in wine which is relatively low in tannin.)

Pinot Noir is the primary grape grown in Burgundy, a cool grape growing area in eastern France (blue area on the map of France). The vineyards of Burgundy are small and are often divided among several growers. Production is very small and thus the best red Burgundies are extremely expensive, although good Burgundy can still be obtained for $35 - $50.

The grape has a reputation for being very hard to grow since it does not tolerate heat well, nor does it like it when things are too cold and damp. However, California and Oregon now produce top quality Pinot Noir, at a fraction of the cost of red Burgundy. If you are looking for quality Pinot Noir and especially if you want good red Burgundy, it is essential to have a good wine merchant to assist you.

Pinot Noir goes with just about any food except Asian cuisine, spicy foods and delicate fish. It is great with salmon, chicken, turkey, pork, ham and beef, and can even be served with lamb or venison, although Cabernet Sauvignon, Syrah or Zinfandel are perhaps better choices with such rich meats.

Grenache

Grenache is a relatively light bodied red wine, usually somewhat lighter in body than Pinot Noir. Although used by itself to make varietal wine, the grapes are often blended with other varieties to make excellent and long lasting red wine in the Southern part of the Rhone Valley in France, and to make Rhone Style blends in California's Central Coast area. It also makes an excellent rosé. In Spain, the wine is known as "Garnacha." The wine goes well with rich fish such as Salmon, as well as with chicken, pork and ham.

Merlot

The area of Bordeaux ("bore doe") in Southwest France, where the Garonne River runs into the sea, has given us two of the most popular wines produced elsewhere in the world - Merlot and Cabernet Sauvignon. Merlot is the primary grape variety grown on the right bank of the Garonne River, and it is used in most of the great wines of the areas of Pomerol and St. Emilion.

The Merlot grape produces medium bodied red wine, which like Pinot Noir is usually lower in tannins than Cabernet Sauvignon. For that reason, it is also frequently used to blend with Cabernet Sauvignon. Merlot goes well with chicken, turkey and most red meat dishes, although some would prefer a heavier bodied wine such as a Cabernet Sauvignon or Syrah, with a steak or roast beef.

Cabernet Sauvignon

Cabernet Sauvignon is the primary grape which produces the most famous wines in the world – the great red wines of the Medoc area of Bordeaux in Southwest France, including Latour, Lafite Rothschild, Mouton Rothschild, Margaux, and Haut Brion. These wines cost hundreds of dollars now in good vintages, but one can obtain Cabernet Sauvignon wines of comparable quality for less than $100 and excellent Cabernet can be had for $20 - $50.

Cabernet Sauvignon is a thick skinned grape which is much easier to grow than Pinot Noir. However it is much higher in tannin, and for that reason Cabernet producers often blend in other varieties to soften the wine, including Merlot, Cabernet Franc, Petit Verdot, and Malbec; so that a red wine from Bordeaux might be 100% Cabernet Sauvignon, or only 60%.

"Claret" is the term the British use to refer to any red wine from Bordeaux. In the United States, a wine which is a blend of at least two of the grape varieties used in Bordeaux, may be authorized by an organization named "Meritage Alliance" to label itself as "Meritage" wine. Thus producers who make a top quality Cabernet Sauvignon blend which is less than 75% Cabernet Sauvignon, may label their wine "Meritage" and are not limited to simply referring to the wine as "red wine."

Cabernet Sauvignon needs some aging in the bottle, in addition to aging in cask, in order to be at its best because otherwise the high tannins mask the fruit flavors of the wine. For that reason, I recommend keeping a small supply of Cabernet in one's cellar for drinking on special occasions.

Cabernet Sauvignon goes best with rich dishes, particularly steak, roast beef, lamb and wild game such as venison. If made in a softer style without too much tannin, or if properly aged, it can even go well with salmon or roasted chicken.

Malbec

Malbec is one of the varieties sometimes used in Bordeaux blends to enhance the flavor of Cabernet Sauvignon, and until recently, it would not even have been considered a major red wine variety. However, a few years ago, vintners in Argentina began producing 100% Malbec of excellent quality, so that it is now the primary varietal made in that country, and some vintners in the United States are now beginning to produce very good Malbec wine.

Malbec is relatively heavy bodied and high in tannin, although most Malbec being produced in Argentina is very drinkable without further aging. Like Cabernet, it goes well with red meat, chicken and lamb.

Syrah / Shiraz

Syrah is an ancient grape thought to have originated in the Middle East, from where it found its way to the Rhone River Valley in Southern France. It is darker than Cabernet Sauvignon, but usually lower in tannin. In the Southern part of the Rhone Valley, Syrah is often blended with several other varieties, including Grenache, to make excellent full bodied red wines, the least expensive of which are usually sold simply as "Cotes du Rhone."

In the Northern part of the Rhone, Syrah is often used exclusively for red wine, including some very expensive wines designated by the village name, such as Hermitage, or even by the name of the vineyard, such as La Landonne.

In Australia, the grape is called Shiraz, and the Australians make excellent Shiraz as well as Shiraz/Cabernet Sauvignon blends.

Syrah is a full bodied wine, dark purple in color, which goes well with steaks, roasts and other red meats, and can even accompany salmon and chicken.

Petite Sirah

Petite Sirah is sometimes confused with Syrah, which was one of its parents when the grape was first created by French botanist François Durif in the 1860's. "Durif" is another name for Petite Sirah, although it is rarely used.

Petite Sirah (the word "petite" referring to the small size of the berries) is very high in tannin and even darker in color than Syrah. Like Syrah and Zinfandel, the grape tolerates heat well and is relatively easy to cultivate, making it popular in California's hotter growing regions.

Petite Sirah's high tannins enable it to age well for many years. The wine goes well with steak and rich beef dishes.

Zinfandel

Zinfandel is a red grape which was given a bad name by using it to make cheap, overly sweet "blush wines" under the name "white Zinfandel." However, Zinfandel made into red wine by leaving the skins in contact with the juice, is an excellent full bodied red, with tannins high enough to warrant some aging in the bottle.

Zinfandel is the same grape believed by some enologists to be "Primitivo" from Southern Italy, but the grapes were probably originally cultivated in Croatia. Zinfandel is relatively easy to grow and tolerates heat, and thus is usually much less expensive than Cabernet Sauvignon or Merlot. It can successfully accompany a variety of dishes, including spaghetti, chicken and red meats.

DESSERT WINES

Dessert wine – sweet wine which is suitable for service after a meal, either by itself or with cheese or fresh fruit – can be made from any grape variety by stopping fermentation before the sugar in the grape juice can be converted to alcohol. Winemaking traditions have resulted in three types of dessert, or sweet, wine which are briefly described below.

Because of the small portions served when having a dessert wine, many of them are bottled in 375ml bottles (half the size of a regular bottle of wine). Although some dessert wines are quite expensive, they can be affordable because they are consumed in such small quantities.

Sparkling Dessert Wine

Any sparkling wine, including Champagne, can be made in a very sweet style suitable for serving with dessert, or as a dessert by itself. This category includes Demi-Sec Champagne,

Asti-Spumante from Italy and other sweet sparkling wines, including excellent sparking Muscat made in the United States.

Sweet Dessert Wine

Sweet dessert wine includes wine made sweet simply by stopping fermentation when there is still a very high level of sugar in the juice, but also includes wine made from grapes which have been left on the vine as long a possible. This often results in a spore called "noble rot" appearing on the grapes, which actually adds flavor and allows the wines to age for many years.

In France, exceptional dessert wines are made in the Sauternes area of Bordeaux, as well as in the Loire Valley and in Alsace. In Germany, wines are labeled according to the level of sugar in sweet wine: Auslese, Beerenauslese and finally Trockenbeerenauslese. A wine called Eiswein is made from grapes which have been left so long on the vine that they have frozen before the harvest.

Fortified Wine

Fortified wine is a third type of sweet wine frequently served after a meal, which is made by adding brandy to the wine, resulting in a wine with very high alcohol levels. Because of the high alcohol, the wine has the ability to age well and tolerate heat. These wines include Port from Portugal, Sherry from Spain, and Madeira from the island of Madeira in the Eastern Atlantic Ocean.

TABLE OF WINE-FOOD PAIRINGS	
FOOD	**SUGGESTED WINE**
Appetizers	**White:** Chenin Blanc, Riesling, Gewürztraminer **Rosé:** dry or semi dry
Sole, Snapper, and Other Delicate Fish, Shellfish	**White:** Chenin Blanc, Pinot Gris, Pinot Blanc, Sauvignon Blanc
Salmon, Light Chicken, Pork	**White:** Pinot Gris, Viognier, Chardonnay, Sauvignon Blanc, Gewürztraminer, Pinot Blanc, **Rosé:** dry **Red:** Grenache, Merlot, Pinot Noir
Ham, Turkey	**White:** Sauvignon Blanc, Chenin Blanc, Riesling, Viognier, Chardonnay, Pinot Blanc, Gewürztraminer, **Rosé:** dry or semi-dry **Red:** Pinot Noir, Grenache, Merlot
Duck, Roasted Chicken	**White:** Viognier, Chardonnay, dry Pinot Blanc, Pinot Gris, **Rosé:** dry, **Red:** Pinot Noir, Grenache, Merlot
Steak, Roast Beef	**Red:** Cabernet Sauvignon, Pinot Noir, Grenache, Merlot, Malbec, Zinfandel Syrah, Petite Sirah
Lamb, Venison, Wild Game	**Red:** Cabernet Sauvignon, Merlot, Malbec, Zinfandel, Syrah, Petite Sirah,
Asian and Spicy Cuisine	**White:** Riesling, Gewürztraminer, Chenin Blanc, **Rosé:** semi-dry

Note that Champagne and other sparkling wines are not included in the above list because Champagne goes well with just about any food.

www.ingramcontent.com/pod-product-compliance
Lightning Source LLC
Chambersburg PA
CBHW022123050726
47591CB00002B/906

* 9 7 8 1 9 5 6 7 3 6 0 7 6 *